THE VIOLENT EARTH

STORM

JENNY WOOD

Thomson Learning
New York

Books in the series

Earthquake
Flood
Storm
Volcano

First published in the
United States in 1993 by
Thomson Learning
115 Fifth Avenue
New York, NY 10003

First published in 1992 by
Wayland (Publishers) Ltd

Cataloging-in-Publication Data applied for

ISBN: 1-56847-002-9

Printed in Italy

Picture: Storm clouds darken the sky over a
beach in England.

CONTENTS

DISASTER!

The storm hits

On November 10, 1970, meteorologists noticed a tropical storm or cyclone developing in the Bay of Bengal, off the coast of East Pakistan (now Bangladesh). On November 13, the storm hit. Violent winds sweeping over the ocean had whipped up a 25-foot tidal wave, a storm surge, which swept over the flat, low-lying land. A newspaper report described how, "...the tidal wave, as high as a two-story building, has changed the map of the delta, sweeping away islands and making others. Whole communities have been destroyed, and all their people and livestock killed."

Survivors of the 1970 cyclone search for personal belongings in what is left of their homes.

The coast of Bangladesh, showing the area that suffered the most severe flooding and the greatest damage during the 1970 cyclone.

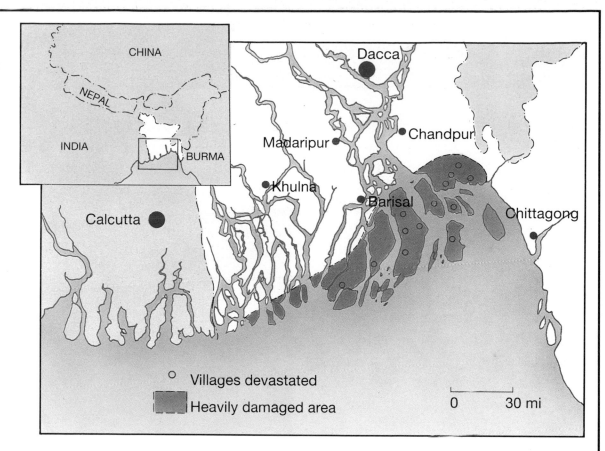

CHINA

NEPAL

INDIA

BURMA

Dacca

Madaripur

Chandpur

Khulna

Barisal

Calcutta

Chittagong

○ Villages devastated

Heavily damaged area

0   30 mi

Tidal wave kills 150,000

The death toll

At the time, the death toll was thought to be 150,000. But the storm hit at harvest time, when there were extra workers in the area, and many of those who survived the storm itself may have died later from hunger or from diseases such as dysentery and typhoid. It is possible, therefore, that as many as one million people may have died–about one-sixth of the area's entire population.

The aftereffects

An international aid effort began immediately. British and American planes flew into the capitol, Dacca, carrying vehicles and helicopters as well as food and medical supplies. The vehicles and helicopters were used to transport the food and medical supplies to the areas that had been completely cut off by the floodwaters.
The British Royal Navy also sent two ships to Dacca, to act as a central base from which the relief effort could be coordinated.

The flat land of Bangladesh has no natural barriers to keep out the sea, and it has been hit by many more natural disasters in recent years.

Huge, gray-black clouds gather on the horizon. Slowly they roll across the sky. Suddenly, the sky glows as a flash of lightning bursts through the darkness. Seconds later, the air echoes with the angry rumbling of thunder. Finally, the rain starts to fall.

Heavy rain, thunder, and lightning are what most people think of when they are asked to describe a storm. A storm is a period of very bad, sometimes violent weather. It may consist of rain, thunder, lightning, hail, snow, strong winds, or any mixture of these.

The storm's damage

Storms occur over both land and sea. Some affect only a small area and last for only a few hours. Others, driven by fierce winds, move across a much wider area and last for days or even weeks. The most severe storms can affect a whole country, sometimes even a whole continent.

Storms can be devastating in their effects. In November 1966, for example, the city of Florence in northern Italy received one-third of its annual rainfall in two days. The Arno River, which flows through Florence, overflows its banks, and muddy

floodwaters poured through the streets. Beside causing chaos in towns, heavy rain can also

damage fields of crops in the countryside.

In very cold conditions, rain turns into snow. Snowstorms can block roads and railroad lines, and make it impossible for people to move around. Strong winds can uproot trees and bring down electricity cables and telephone lines. Some winds are so powerful that they can flatten buildings and destroy whole towns. During the very worst storms, many people are killed.

A summer storm over Tucson, Arizona. Bright flashes of lightning illuminate the night sky.

A LOOK AT WEATHER

Weather is the state or condition of the air in the troposphere (the lowest level of the atmosphere) at a particular time. But the condition of the air is constantly changing, and so the weather changes too, from hot to cold, dry to wet, and calm to windy.

Changes in the weather
Weather changes occur, first of all, because the temperature of the air changes. As the sun's rays warm the surface of the earth, heat is released into the troposphere. This heat, in turn, warms up the air around it.

Moisture released into the troposphere returns to the earth in the form of rain, hail, and snow.

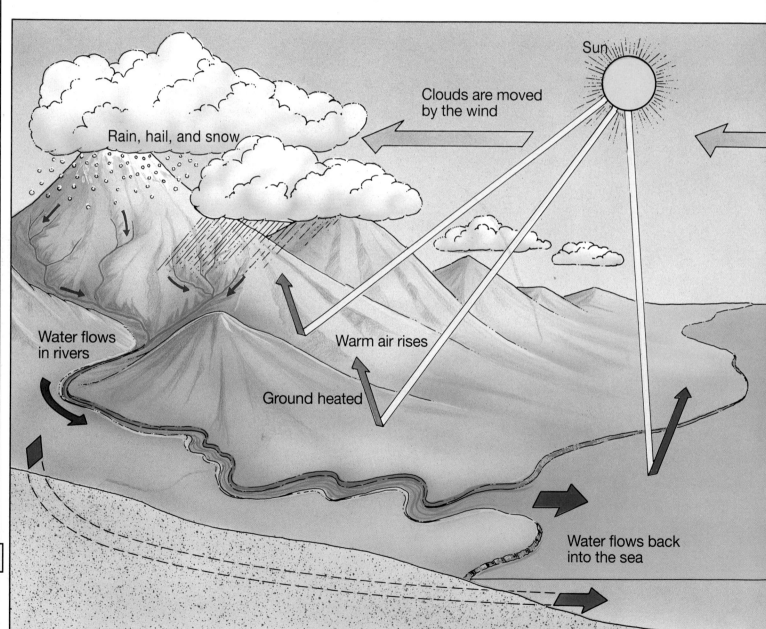

Sun

Clouds are moved by the wind

Rain, hail, and snow

Warm air rises

Water flows in rivers

Ground heated

Water flows back into the sea

When a cold air mass meets a warm air mass, a depression forms and storms occur. The diagram (right) shows a cross section of the area marked A-B on the inset.

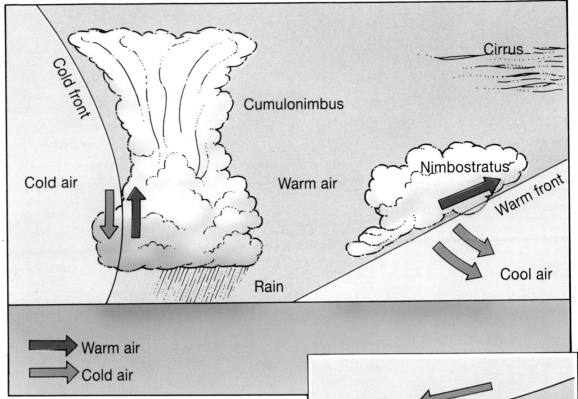

Cold front

Cold air

Cumulonimbus

Warm air

Cirrus

Nimbostratus

Warm front

Cool air

Rain

→ Warm air

⇒ Cold air

Moisture in the air forms clouds

Water evaporates from the sea

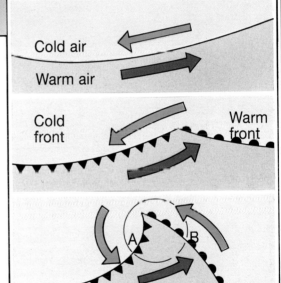

Cold air

Warm air

Cold front

Warm front

A B

But warm air rises and, as the warm air drifts upward, cold air sweeps in to take its place. So large masses of warm and cold air constantly jostle for position, creating winds and changes in temperature.

The amount of moisture in the air affects the weather too. The sun's rays cause moisture to be released from seas and rivers into the troposphere. Air can hold a certain amount of moisture, but when it reaches its limit, any extra moisture condenses into water droplets, and clouds form. These water droplets may eventually fall as rain, hail, or snow. Warm air can hold more moisture than cold air, so as the air cools, rain, hail, or snow are more likely to occur.

How storms occur

Storms occur when cold and warm air masses meet. The air masses do not mix, and clouds form along the edge, or "front." The greater the difference in temperature between the two air masses, and the larger the air masses are, the more violent the storms are likely to be.

9

THUNDERSTORMS

At any time, about 1,800 thunderstorms are happening throughout the world. Thunderstorms are the most common type of storm.

They usually occur when the air is warm and damp. As the warm air rises, it cools down, and the moisture it contains forms clouds.

Lightning occurs when negative electrical charges flow toward positive charges, or vice versa.

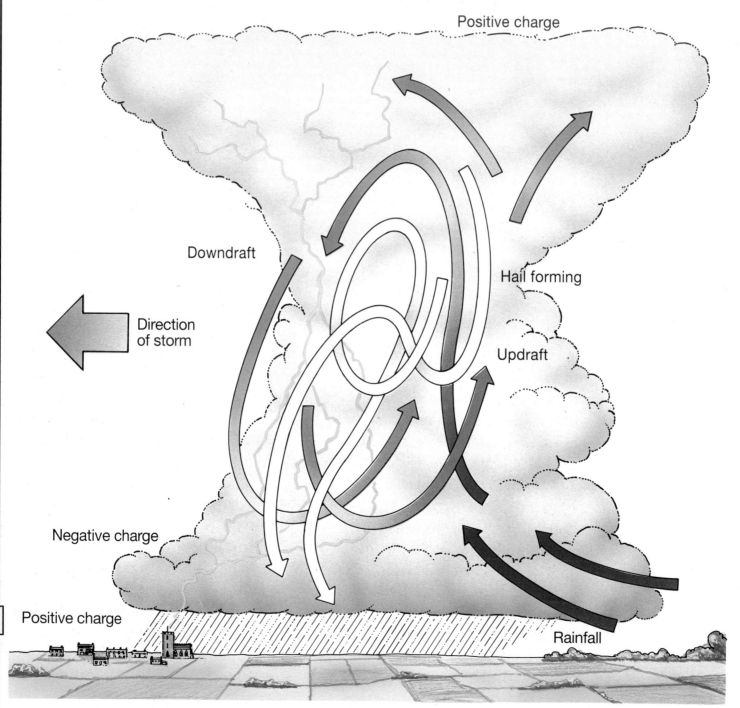

Positive charge

Downdraft

Direction of storm

Hail forming

Updraft

Negative charge

Positive charge

Rainfall

A thundercloud producing very heavy rainfall in Australia. Rainstorms may cover only a small area, but they can cause severe flooding.

Thunderclouds

The clouds that build up to produce thunderstorms are called cumulonimbus. They are huge gray-black clouds, which can stretch so high into the atmosphere that the water droplets in the tops of the clouds turn into ice crystals. Usually these ice crystals melt to form raindrops, but when the crystals remain frozen they eventually fall as hailstones.

Lightning

Inside a cumulonimbus cloud, fast-moving currents of air rise and fall, tossing the water droplets and ice crystals around violently. This furious movement causes electric charges to build up within the cloud. Eventually, these charges become so strong that the electricity is released in the form of a giant spark, which we know as lightning.

Thunder

Lightning heats the air in its path to about 60,000°F—five times hotter than the surface of the sun! The heated air expands quickly. As it does so, it collides with the surrounding cool air. This collision of hot and cold air produces sound waves that we hear as thunder.

Thunder and lightning always occur together, at exactly the same time. But because light travels faster than sound, we always see lightning before we hear thunder. The amount of time between a flash of lightning and a clap of thunder tells you how far away the thunderstorm is. Every five seconds counts as a little over a mile.

11

SNOWSTORMS

A fall of snow can look beautiful, but as little as 4 inches of snow lying on the ground is enough to cause chaos. Snow can block roads, bring down telephone lines and electric cables, and maroon people in their homes.

"...the manner in which snow often arrives in a blizzard, or departs by avalanche or thaw flood, means that snow must be considered a treacherous enemy." (I. Holford, British author of a book on weather.)

The cause of snowstorms

Snowstorms occur when a mass of freezing air moves out from the polar regions. When it meets a mass of warm air, the warm air rises quickly, and a heavy snowstorm usually occurs. Snow falls from a cloud only if the temperature of the air between the base of the cloud and the ground is below about 40°F. If the temperature is higher, the snowflakes will melt as they travel through the air and fall as rain or sleet.

When icy polar air meets a warm air mass, the cold air undercuts the warm air ahead. A huge bank of clouds forms, bringing heavy snowfall.

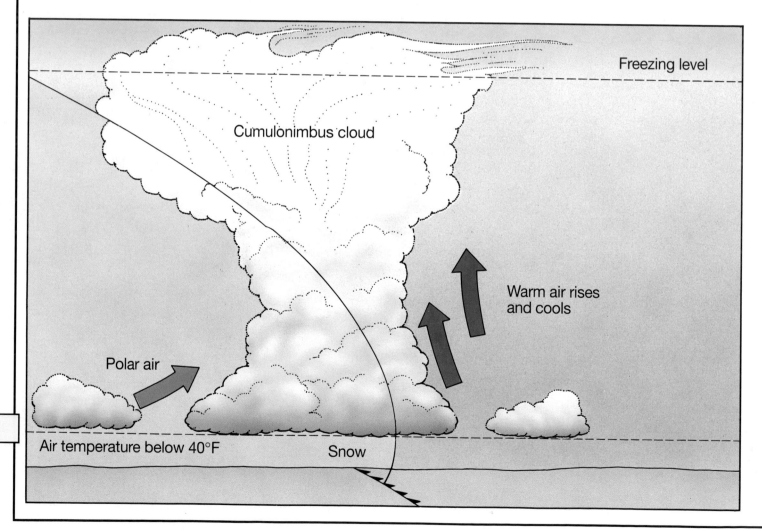

Freezing level

Cumulonimbus cloud

Warm air rises and cools

Polar air

Air temperature below 40°F

Snow

Although all snowflakes have six sides, they vary in shape and size. One snowflake may consist of as many as 100 ice crystals and be over an inch in diameter.

A snowplow is being used to clear snow from roads after a heavy snowstorm.

The formation of snowflakes
Snowflakes are produced when ice crystals in a cloud collide and stick together. All snowflakes have six sides, but of all the billions of snowflakes that have fallen on the earth, it seems that no two are exactly alike. The different shapes reflect the different weather conditions in which they are produced. Needle and rod shapes form in very cold air. More complicated patterns form in warmer air.

Blizzards
The worst kind of snowstorm is called a blizzard. During a blizzard, strong winds blow the snow into huge piles called snowdrifts, which can bury farm animals and cars, and prevent people from moving out of their homes for days at a time. It is dangerous to travel during a blizzard, as the air temperature may be 10°F or lower, and visibility less than 400-500 feet.

DUST STORMS AND SANDSTORMS

Dust storms
Dust storms occur in places where the soil is very dry and has no vegetation to anchor and protect it. Fierce winds blow across the land, lifting the dry, dusty soil high into the air and carrying it away. After a severe dust storm, it may be impossible to grow crops on the land for a number of years.

Below: An American family, affected by the terrible "Dust Bowl" droughts of the 1930s, prays for rain.

"When the night came again it was black night, for the stars could not pierce the dust to get down, and the window lights could not even spread beyond their own yards. Now the dust was evenly mixed with the air.... Houses were shut tight, and cloths wedged around doors and windows....In the morning the dust hung like fog, and the sun was as red as ripe new blood." (A passage from The Grapes of Wrath *by John Steinbeck.)*

The Dust Bowl
By the early 1900s, many people had settled in the Midwest in the United States and had begun to farm the fertile land. Soon, the midwestern states became one of the world's largest wheat-growing areas, nicknamed "the bread basket of America."

At the beginning of the 1930s, heat waves and drought began to dry up the soil. Then, in 1934, came the first great dust storm. Fierce winds whipped up the

Travelers struggling across the desert during a sandstorm in Cameroon, West Africa.

loose top layer of soil and carried over 300 million tons of dirt all the way to the East Coast. The dust storms continued, over forty of them occurring in 1935 alone. It became impossible to farm the land, now known as the Dust Bowl, and thousands of bankrupt farmers and their families had no choice but to move west toward California in search of whatever work they could find.

Sandstorms

Most sandstorms occur in dry, desert areas. Strong winds whisk up the loose top layer of sand and carry it through the air. The swirling sand forms a low cloud about 20 inches above the ground. The sand moves erratically, as the grains collide. Sandstorms are dangerous to desert travelers. People cannot see, and they lose their sense of direction. Sandstorms can also damage crops and clog up machinery.

A tornado is a type of violent whirlwind. This whirlwind is a column of air that spins across an area of land at tremendous speed, causing terrible damage to anything in its path. Tornadoes are usually accompanied by heavy rain, thunder, and lightning. Most tornadoes occur in the Midwest and South of the United States.

How a tornado forms

A tornado forms over land when a mass of cool, dry air collides with a mass of warm, damp air coming from the opposite direction. Cumulonimbus clouds form along the front or "squall line" where the two air masses meet. The warm air rises very quickly. As it does so, more warm air rushes in to take its place. This air also rises, and begins to rotate in the base of the cloud. The rotating air then spirals downward from the cloud, in the shape of a funnel. A hissing sound can be heard as the funnel moves toward the earth. If the funnel reaches the ground, it raises a cloud of dust and debris. The hissing becomes a roar. Then the tornado whirls across the land, sweeping up objects and destroying almost everything in its path.

A tornado's speed

Most tornadoes travel over an area of about 20 miles, at speeds from 10 to 25 miles per hour. But some travel ten times that distance, at 60 miles an hour or more. The speed of the winds whirling around the center of the storm is difficult to measure, because the tornado usually destroys everything in sight, including instruments set up to record its progress, but estimates range from 200 to 600 miles per hour.

The distinctive funnel cloud of a tornado spirals toward the ground.

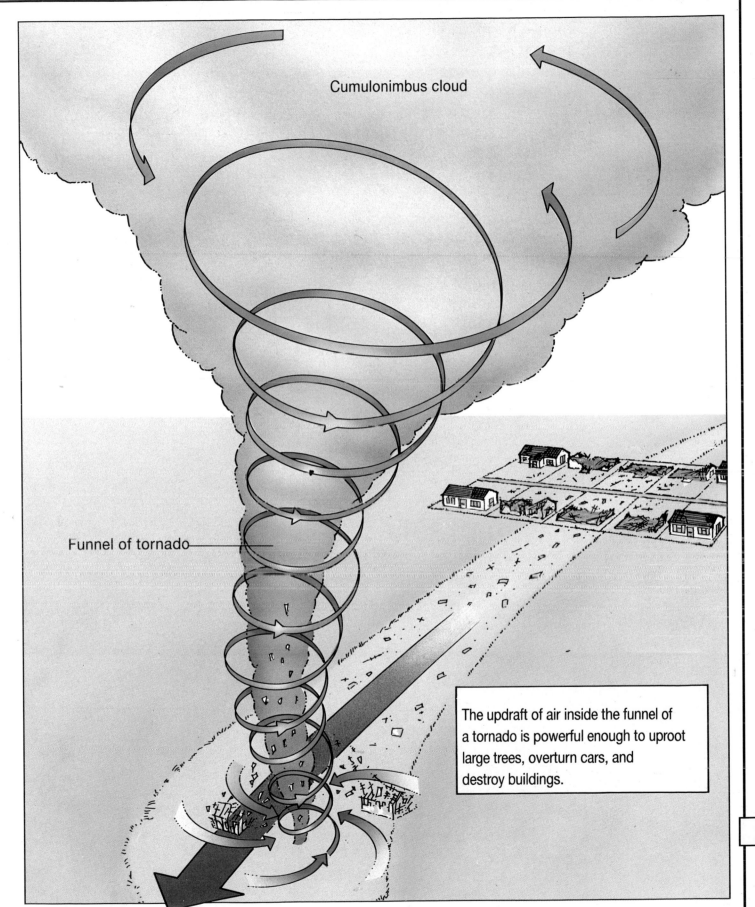

Cumulonimbus cloud

Funnel of tornado

The updraft of air inside the funnel of a tornado is powerful enough to uproot large trees, overturn cars, and destroy buildings.

About 700 tornadoes or "twisters" as they are frequently called, are reported each year in the United States. Most occur in the spring, in the afternoon or evening of a hot, humid day.

Advance warning

Scientists of the National Weather Service constantly gather reports from weather stations all over the country. If a tornado is likely to develop, the Service broadcasts this information on television and radio. When a tornado is spotted, the Service issues a warning to all the communities likely to lie in the tornado's path. The inhabitants of many tornado-hit areas have learned over the years where to take cover. Some have even built special underground storm cellars in which to take shelter until the danger is past.

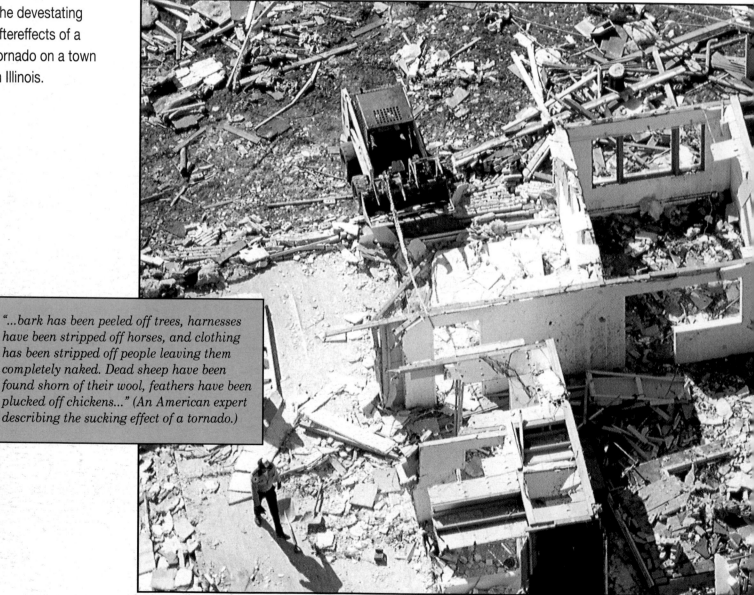

The devestating aftereffects of a tornado on a town in Illinois.

"...bark has been peeled off trees, harnesses have been stripped off horses, and clothing has been stripped off people leaving them completely naked. Dead sheep have been found shorn of their wool, feathers have been plucked off chickens..." (An American expert describing the sucking effect of a tornado.)

Disaster strikes!

On April 2 and 3, 1974, more than 100 tornadoes roared across a vast area of the United States from Alabama and Georgia in the south, through Ohio and Kentucky farther north, right across the Canadian border into Ontario. Many of the areas lay outside the usual tornado belt and were unused to such fierce storms.

In a period of eight hours, over 300 people were killed and hundreds more injured. Damage to property was estimated at hundreds of millions of dollars. Three-quarters of the buildings in a town in Kentucky were demolished. In Ohio, the top floor of a high school was blown away. Guin, a small town in Alabama, completely disappeared. "Guin just isn't there," said a state trooper when the extent of the storm damage became apparent.

HURRICANES

Like a tornado, a hurricane is a powerful, whirling windstorm, but hurricanes form over warm ocean water, not over land. Hurricanes are much larger than tornadoes, and can measure as much as 300 miles in diameter. A hurricane may last for hours, sometimes for days, and can travel a great distance across the ocean and over land. Hurricanes that form over the Pacific Ocean are often called typhoons or cyclones.

Formation of hurricanes
Hurricanes develop over the warm seas on either side of the equator at times when the air is moist and the temperature is over 80°F. As these sea heats the air, a current of warm, moist air rises above the water. Winds rush in below this air current and whirl upward. As they rise, they cool, and the huge amounts of water vapor they contain form towering storm clouds. At the center of a hurricane is a calm area known as the eye. Surrounding the eye are "wall clouds" where the strongest winds (up to 180 miles per hour) and heaviest rain occur.

The path of a hurricane
As a hurricane moves over the ocean, it stirs up huge waves on the surface of the sea.

If these waves reach land, they cause immense damage, flooding coastal towns and killing many people.

When a hurricane moves over land, strong winds and heavy rain batter the area for several hours and may cause devastation. Then, as the eye passes over the area, there is a brief period of calm until the winds on the other side of the hurricane arrive, causing more destruction.

A hurricane needs warm, moist air from the sea to give it energy. As the hurricane moves over land, it begins to die down very gradually.

Right: This photograph, taken over the Gulf of Mexico in August 1980, shows clearly the circular shape of a hurricane and the eye at its center.

Below: Because of pressure changes, the air in the eye of a hurricane does not rise, although it is warmer than the air in the rest of the storm. Instead, the air sinks downard.

20

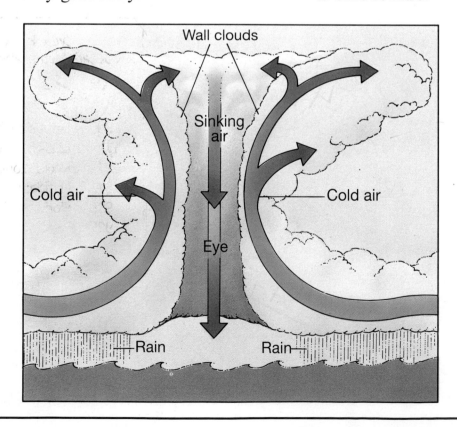
Wall clouds
Sinking air
Cold air
Cold air
Eye
Rain
Rain

Some severe hurricanes in the United States that have caused deaths (since 1900)

Date	Area	Deaths
1900	Galveston, Texas	6,000
1909	Louisiana; Mississippi	350
1915	Texas; Louisiana	275
1919	Florida; Louisiana; Texas	285
1926	Florida; Alabama	240
1928	Florida	1,800
1935	Florida	400
1938	Long Island; southern New England	600
1957	Louisiana; Mississippi; Texas (Audrey*)	450
1969	Louisiana; Virginia (Camille*)	250
1992	Florida; Louisiana (Andrew*)	33

*since the 1950s, hurricanes have been identified by names

STORM-HIT COUNTRIES

Many areas of the world are regularly hit by severe storms, often with devastating effects.

The United States

The United States, the world's fourth largest country, suffers heavy rainstorms, snowstorms, hurricanes, tornadoes, and dust storms, all causing great damage and loss of life. The midwestern and southern states are frequently hit by tornadoes, while areas near the Atlantic Ocean and the Gulf of Mexico are affected by hurricanes.

Buildings and land still suffer terrible storm damage but advance warning systems in the U.S. now save many people's lives.

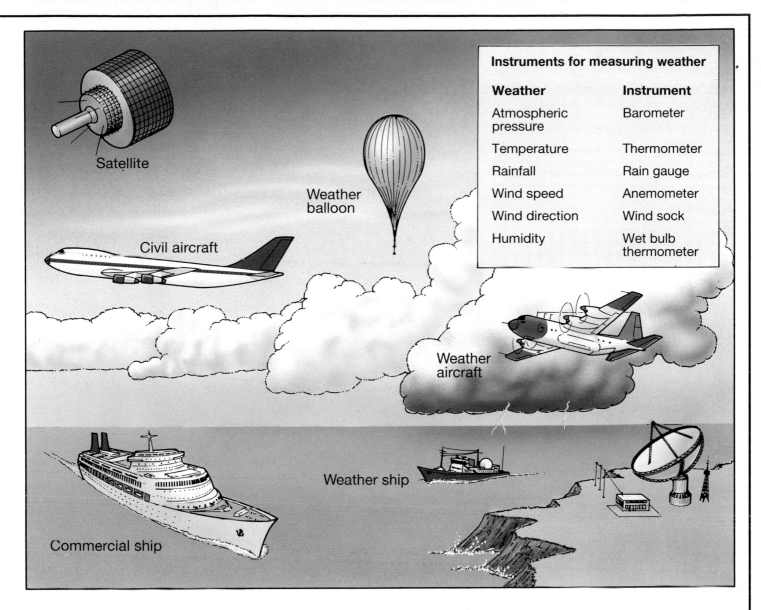

Satellite

Weather balloon

Civil aircraft

Weather aircraft

Weather ship

Commercial ship

Instruments for measuring weather	
Weather	**Instrument**
Atmospheric pressure	Barometer
Temperature	Thermometer
Rainfall	Rain gauge
Wind speed	Anemometer
Wind direction	Wind sock
Humidity	Wet bulb thermometer

This diagram shows some of the ways that weather forecasters gather information and collect data about the condition of the atmosphere.

The area around the Great Lakes, and New England often receive such heavy snowfall that the land is covered with snow for between 90 and 140 days each year.

Warning in advance
In many ways, however, the people of the United States are fortunate. Storm-warning systems are now highly efficient. Meteorologists examine photographs taken by weather satellites and collect information on wind speeds and temperature. The data can warn them of bad weather, so people are frequently able to flee an area before a storm strikes. Many people have their own cars, too, which makes evacuation easier. Some people can afford to build storm shelters, and architects have developed ways of strengthening buildings to withstand storm damage. The numbers of deaths associated with natural disasters has decreased steadily in the United States over the last 50 years.

Developing countries

Poorer countries are not so fortunate. In places such as Bangladesh, the Philippines, and Taiwan, even if storm warnings are given well in advance, most people just have to sit tight and hope that they will survive. Few have their own cars or trucks, and houses are often built of wood or other natural materials that cannot withstand the force of a tropical storm. Many of these countries are low lying, while others are islands, so they have little or no protection against the power of a storm-swept sea. Death tolls are often huge, and the survivors often find it impossible to scratch a living from the devastated land.

Hurricane Fifi

On September 18, 1974, the Central American country of Honduras was hit by Hurricane Fifi. The hurricane arrived in the middle of the night, sweeping away houses, roads, bridges, and railroad tracks. The torrential rain caused rivers to flood. In the city of San Pedro Sula, 400,000 people were left homeless and without food.

Even before the hurricane struck, Honduras was a poor country, struggling for survival. Its economy depended on its main exports, bananas, sugar, and coffee. Banana crops were completely destroyed, and other crops, including food crops, were badly damaged. Many people

Satellite photographs are used to monitor the development of tropical storms. But it is not always possible for people to escape before the storm arrives.

Survivors of Hurricane Fifi among the ruins of their home.

starved to death. Overseas aid was provided, but the effects of the hurricane on such a poor country were terrible and long-lasting.

"This is all that is left of our beautiful house. It had a veranda, fruit trees and looked on to the river. Now all is lost." (A 74-year-old carpenter who survived a hurricane with his wife.)

Meteorologists in Canada gathering information on temperature and wind speed.

Weather forecasting is important in many ways to all sorts of people. Facts and figures about the weather are recorded constantly by weather stations all around the world.

This information is sent to meteorologists in weather forecasting centers, who use computers to help them analyze the information. The computers print out maps that show how weather conditions are likely to change over the following days and weeks.

Weather forecasting equipment
Besides computers, many other sophisticated instruments now help meteorologists find out about the weather. Weather satellites are able to take photographs of earth from high up in the atmosphere.
These photographs provide valuable information about the progress of storms. Meteorologists use radar, too, to help them make more accurate weather forecasts. Radar pictures can show the position of rain, snow, and hail. An experienced forecaster can use this information to make weather predictions.

Controlling the weather
It is very unlikely that scientists will ever be able to control the weather, but they are experimenting with ways of altering weather conditions on a small scale. One of these ways is called cloud seeding. Chemicals

are sprayed or dropped into clouds to trigger rainfall. Cloud seeding is most often used to produce rain over very dry areas, but it can also be used to reduce the strength of a storm. This includes lessening the possible damage caused by lightning and heavy hailstones. As rainfall is released from the cloud, the storm's energy fades.

Advance warning
Perhaps the most important achievement in weather forecasting to date is the ability of meteorologists to give accurate advance warning of storms. Disasters do still occur, but predictions of hurricanes, tornadoes, and floods have, on many occasions, saved thousands of lives.

Computers help meteorologists make accurate predictions about the weather.

27

1. Making an electric charge

Lightning is caused by static electricity. Electric charges build up in the air until they are discharged. A flash of lightning is a huge discharge of electricity. You can make static electricity by rubbing together a comb and a piece of wool or nylon cloth. When the comb is charged with static electricity, it can pull at things the way a magnet does. This is why pieces of paper become attached to the comb. Once they are attached, the pull stops, and eventually the paper falls off. This means the electric charge has gone.

Materials:
A comb
A piece of paper
Scissors
A piece of wool or nylon cloth

Method:

1. Cut the sheet of paper into small pieces.

2. Rub the cloth with the comb, using strong, quick movements.

3. Hold the comb near the pieces of paper. The paper will be attracted to the comb.

Another way of demonstrating static electricity is by rubbing a comb on a wool sweater then holding the comb near a friend's hair. Watch what happens. Some of the hair should rise up toward the comb.

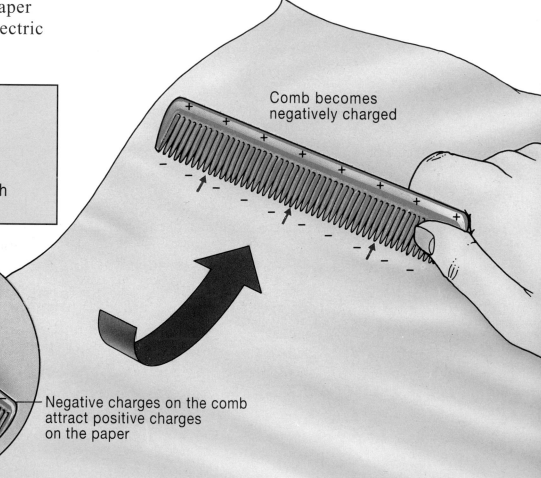

Comb becomes negatively charged

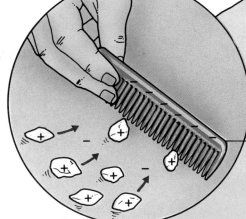

Negative charges on the comb attract positive charges on the paper

2. Measuring the wind

Meteorologists measure the speed of the wind using an instrument called an anemometer. The most common type of anemometer has three or four cups attached to spokes on a rotating shaft. As the wind blows, the spokes turn the shaft. The speed of the wind is indicated by the speed of the spinning shaft. Try making a simple type of anemometer that turns in the wind.

Materials:
A piece of cardboard
A pencil
Scissors
Strong paper
3 jar tops
Scotch tape
A strip of red paper

Method:

1. Roll up strips of paper to make three tubes of equal length. Make one shorter, fatter paper tube, too.

2. Draw a circle on the cardboard and cut it out. Attach the short paper tube to the base of the cardboard with tape.

3. Tape each of the longer tubes to one of the jar tops. Now tape the tubes to the underside of the cardboard circle, spacing them out evenly. Attach the strip of red paper to one lid.

4. Insert the pencil into the short paper tube, and make sure that the cardboard circle spins easily.

5. Take your measuring instrument outside. Hold it up and allow it to turn freely in the wind. Count how many turns the red marker makes in one minute. Repeat this test in the same way at the same time each day for a week. Keep a record of your findings.

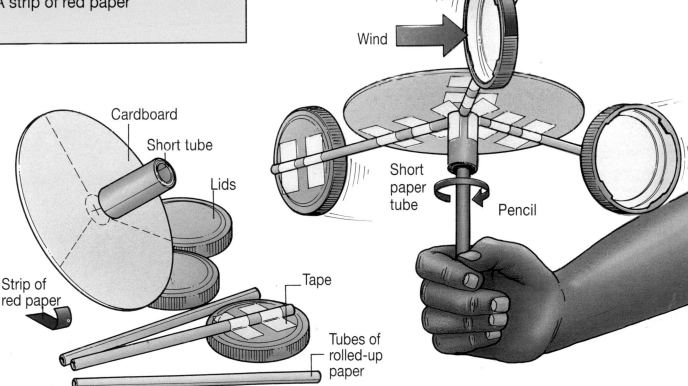

Cardboard

Short tube

Lids

Strip of red paper

Tape

Tubes of rolled-up paper

Wind

Short paper tube

Pencil

GLOSSARY

AIR CURRENT A movement of air.

AIR MASS A very large area of air with the same temperature throughout.

ATMOSPHERE The thin blanket of air that surrounds the earth.

CUMULONIMBUS A very large thundercloud that brings heavy rain, hail, or snow.

DEATH TOLL The total number of people who die as a result of a disaster.

DELTA A triangular area of swampy land created where the mouth of a river branches into several streams.

DYSENTERY An infection of the intestine caused by drinking polluted water.

EVACUATION The movement of people out of an area because of war or disaster.

EYE The calm, cloudless area at the center of a hurricane.

FRONT The edge of an air mass.

HAILSTONES Small pellets of ice that fall from cumulonimbus clouds.

METEOROLOGIST A scientist who studies the weather.

NATURAL DISASTER Any terrible event, not caused by human activity, that results in deaths, injuries, or damage to property.

RADAR A system that locates distant objects by sending out radio waves and detecting them when they bounce back off the objects.

SLEET Falling snow or hail that has partly melted; partly frozen rain.

TROPOSPHERE The lower layer of the atmosphere where most weather occurs.

TYPHOID A dangerous infectious fever caused by drinking polluted water.

VEGETATION All the trees and plants that grow in a particular area.

VISIBILITY The distance over which objects can be seen.

WALL CLOUDS Heavy clouds that form around the eye of a hurricane.

WEATHER SATELLITE A device that orbits the earth and sends back scientific information about the weather.

BOOKS TO READ

Archer, Jules. *Hurricane!* Nature's Disasters. New York: Crestwood House, 1991.

Archer, Jules. *Tornado!* Nature's Disasters. New York: Crestwood House, 1991.

Dineen, Jacqueline. *Hurricanes and Typhoons*. Natural Disasters. New York: Franklin Watts, 1991.

Dixon, Dougal. *The Changing Earth*. Young Geographer. Thomson Learning, 1993.

Knapp, Brian. *Storm*. World Disasters. Austin: Steck-Vaughn, 1990.

Steele, Philip. *Storms: Causes and Effects*. Weather Watch. New York: Franklin Watts, 1991.

Twist, Clint. *Hurricanes and Storms*. Repairing the Damage. New York: New Discovery, 1992.

Picture acknowledgments

The publishers would like to thank the following for allowing their photographs to be reproduced in this book: Camera Press 4 (Gus Coral); the Hutchison Library (Val & Alan Wilkinson) 14/15; J. Allan Cash Ltd 2/3; Frank Lane Picture Agency 22; Rex Features (Matthew Naythons/Sipa Press) 25; Science Photo Library *cover* (Keith Kent), 6/7 (Ken Wood), 11 (Gordon Gerradd), 21 (Hasler & Pierce NASA GSFC), 24 (NOAA), 26 (Stephen Krasemann); Tony Stone Worldwide 13 (bottom); Topham Picture Library 14 (bottom), 16; Zefa Picture Library 13 top (Dr F. Sauer), 18/19, 27 (B. Harris).

Permission to print an extract from *The Grapes of Wrath* by John Steinbeck is by courtesy of William Heinemann Ltd.

INDEX